The New Charter for Children's Play

Children's Play Council

children's play council

national children's bureau
making a difference

The Children's Society

Contents

	Introduction	3
1	Children	7
2	Parents and carers	8
3	Play for all	9
4	Neighbourhood play	10
5	Play strategies	11
6	Play services	12
7	Schools and play	13
8	Safe play	14
9	Special play situations	15
10	Playwork education and training	16
	References and further reading	17

Introduction

Play today

Children need and want to play, indoors and out, in whatever way they can. Through playing, children develop their abilities, explore their creativity and learn about themselves, other people and the world around them. Children have the right to play – as stated in the United Nations Convention on the Rights of the Child (see page 4), ratified by the United Kingdom in 1991. Children, who make up nearly a quarter of the population, have a right to expect their play needs to be taken into account. Moreover, play can itself help agencies to achieve broader, strategic goals – such as developing and sustaining healthy, safe communities, combating social exclusion and improving people's living environments. So supporting children's play is both a duty and an opportunity.

Barriers to play

Children of all ages play, but a great many children lack adequate or appropriate play opportunities. Children whose play opportunities are restricted or denied, for whatever reason, can suffer developmentally and the communities and families they live in are impoverished as a result.

Children's opportunities to play are often restricted by factors such as discrimination, inappropriate responses to disability and special needs, insufficient space, environmental dangers, poverty and other social conditions, fears for children's safety, individual or family circumstances. Many children lack access to good quality play opportunities because of the failure of central and local government to recognise the importance of play. This failure has two consequences: first, many public services and functions ignore or downplay children's play needs, and second, insufficient financial resources are directed towards services that specifically aim to improve opportunities for children to play.

Aims of the Charter

The New Charter for Children's Play sets out a vision for play. Developing the themes of the 1989 United Nations Convention on the Rights of the Child, and especially Article 31 on the child's right to play, the Charter acts as a catalyst for organisations to examine, review and improve their services, activities and functions in the light of children's play needs.

The Charter is also an effective campaigning tool for individuals and organisations working to raise awareness of the importance of play and to stimulate better play opportunities, at local, regional or national level.

Article 31 of the United Nations Convention on the Rights of the Child states:

1. States Parties recognize the right of the child to rest and leisure, to engage in play and recreational activities appropriate to the age of the child and to participate freely in cultural life and the arts.

2. States Parties shall respect and promote the right of the child to participate fully in cultural and artistic life and shall encourage the provision of appropriate and equal opportunities for cultural artistic, recreational and leisure activity.

Using the Charter

The Charter presents many opportunities for organisations and individuals that wish to take action to improve children's opportunities to play. Organisations whose services impact on children's play, such as local authorities, voluntary organisations, health, education and social service providers can implement the Charter in the following ways:

★ Formally adopt the Charter at elected member/governing body level in order to raise awareness of the importance of play. A suitable resolution would be: 'to promote the aims and objectives of *The New Charter for Children's Play*, and to work to ensure that policies and practices across the organisation support and promote children's access to a range of play opportunities and services'.

★ Use the Charter as the basis for strategic planning of services as they relate to play.

★ Use the Charter as a checklist to review all services and functions that have an effect on children's play.

Children and young people, parents, community groups, play associations, and politicians can use the Charter to support their work to create better play opportunities in their areas, for instance by pressing relevant agencies to adopt it.

The Children's Play Council's definition of play

The Children's Play Council defines play in the following way:

Play is an essential part of every child's life and vital to their development. It is the way children explore the world around them and develop and practise skills. It is essential for physical, emotional and spiritual growth, for intellectual and educational development, and for acquiring social and behavioural skills. Play is a generic term applied to a wide range of activities and behaviours that are satisfying to the child, creative for the child and freely chosen by the child. Children's play may or may not involve equipment or have an end product. Children play on their own and with others. Their play may be boisterous and energetic or quiet and contemplative, light-hearted or very serious.

The benefits of play

★ Play promotes children's development, learning, creativity and independence.

★ Play keeps children healthy and active – active children become active adults.

★ Play fosters social inclusion. It helps children understand the people and places in their lives, learn about their environment and develop their sense of community.

★ Play allows children to find out about themselves, their abilities and their interests.

★ Play is therapeutic. It helps children to deal with difficult or painful circumstances, such as emotional stress or medical treatment.

★ Play gives children the chance to let off steam and have fun.

The Children's Play Council

The Children's Play Council aims to raise awareness of the importance of play in children's lives and to stimulate better play opportunities and play services. The Council is committed to achieving the full implementation of *The New Charter for Children's Play* and Article 31 of the United Nations Convention on the Rights of the Child.

The Council's work reaches wherever children play: at home, in play areas, parks, school playgrounds and streets, in play and childcare centres, in hospitals and community health settings, in cities and in the countryside.

The Council operates under the aegis of the National Children's Bureau.

The Children's Society

The Children's Society is one of Britain's leading charities for children and young people. It works with children of all ages, their families and communities, to help give young people a better chance in life.

The Society believes that all children, whatever their culture or social background, should have a good start. An important means of achieving this is through play. Children learn vital life skills and develop their understanding of the world through play. They need to experience play in safe stimulating environments, both within their homes and in their communities.

Play nurtures the spiritual, physical, intellectual, emotional and social development of children. The Children's Society calls on agencies to work together to ensure equal access and opportunity for all children.

Children

All children need to play and have a right to play. Children of all ages should be able to play freely and confidently on their own and with other children.

Action point for adults
★ Ensure that children and young people have the opportunity to play and take part in a range of activities where they can gain confidence and learn on their own terms.

Action points for play services
★ Support and encourage children's own ideas and decisions about what they do and how they do it.

★ Respect and value all children. Ensure that they can play free from racial or other types of harassment or abuse – from other children or from adults.

★ Enable children to express their views – and take their views into account. However, do challenge children when they express views or act to the detriment of others.

★ Provide opportunities for children to be involved in the planning and organisation of programmes and activities.

Action point for other services
★ Support children's play and respect the right of the child to free play and self-determination through other children's activities as well. This includes education, childcare, art, sport, leisure and recreational activities.

'Children should show respect to other children's games.' (Nicola Duff, age 11)

'Racism, bullying and fears for personal safety are the main reasons stated by Bangladeshi children for not using their local play centres.' (Howarth, 1997)

2 Parents and carers

Parents and other carers should respect and value their children's play and try to maximise their opportunities for safe and stimulating play within and outside the home.

Action point for parents and carers
★ Make time to play and take part in recreational activities with your children - at all ages and stages of their development. This is a fundamental aspect of good parenting.

Action points for play services
★ Encourage parents and other carers to support their children's play and enrich the home play environment in creative ways which are safe and inexpensive.

★ Recognise that there may be cultural and other variations in play in the home environment.

★ Where parents are involved in managing and for delivering play services or activities, give them sufficient support to enable them to do this effectively.

★ Consult with, and provide information for, parents and children about play services and opportunities in their areas, and about shaping their local environment.

'I think it's sometimes a bit harder for older people to play because they lose their imagination.' (Matthew Katz, age 7)

Play for all

All children should have equal access to play opportunities and services.

Action points for service planners

★ Ensure that the same range of play services and opportunities are equally available and accessible to disabled and non-disabled children.

★ Give children of all ages, from the early years, through the middle years and right into young adulthood, access to appropriate play opportunities.

★ Take account of children's different abilities, their age, gender, cultural backgrounds, social, family, economic and environmental situations.

★ Value and respect the different religions, cultures, languages and abilities in our society. Treat each child as an individual without stereotyping.

Action points for play professionals

★ Enable children to develop positive attitudes to differences of ethnicity, religion, culture, language, gender and ability.

★ Develop equal opportunities policies which apply to management, employment practice, training, access to services, service delivery, equipment and resources.

'Everyday opportunities for Bangladeshi children to play were limited by incidents of bullying, racism and fears for their personal safety.' (Howarth, 1997)

4 Neighbourhood play

All children should be able to play safely outdoors wherever they live, in cities and in the countryside. Older children should also be able to get around safely on their own.

Action points for politicians

★ Extend and safeguard children's safe access to the countryside, to open spaces and natural areas wherever they live.

★ Promote walking and cycling – modes of travel that are particularly important for children's mobility.

★ Wherever possible, put the needs of children before the needs of motorists in residential streets.

★ Make wider use of traffic calming, home zones and other measures to reduce levels of motorised traffic in residential areas.

Action points for planners and architects

★ Give children access to the whole environment, not just to designated play areas. Allow children to play in the everyday environments of cities, towns, villages and the countryside.

★ Consider and cater for children's play needs throughout public spaces, in new housing developments, environmental and road schemes, as well as public facilities such as clinics, libraries and shopping areas.

★ Enable children and young people to participate in the planning of local recreational facilities and public spaces, and respond to their needs and views.

★ Adapt and improve existing areas with inadequate play facilities to take into account children's needs for good quality, safe play opportunities.

★ Replace 'no ball games' signs with 'we welcome play' signs wherever possible.

'My neighbourhood is not very safe because cars speed up and down. It is in fact a side road but it links two major roads. It would be better if there were speed bumps.' (David Guard, age 11)

Play strategies

Central and local government and voluntary organisations should think creatively and strategically about children and their play needs.

Action points for politicians
★ Acknowledge the importance of providing play services and opportunities for all children and allocate sufficient funding to play.

★ Work in partnership with the voluntary sector and with parents, to provide a range of play services and opportunities which meet the needs of all children and families.

★ Help set up and support play forums which aim to improve and coordinate local, regional and national play services and opportunities.

Action points for public bodies with responsibility for play
★ Develop play policies and strategies aimed at achieving full implementation of Article 31 of the United Nations Convention on the Rights of the Child (see page 4).

★ Develop national minimum standards for play services and play provision covering both quality and quantity for children of all ages.

Action point for play services
★ Develop effective management and play development strategies to ensure the delivery of high quality play services.

'Our children's committee went to the Town Hall and we told the councillors why we need to keep our play centres. We won, the cuts didn't come.' (Member of the children's committee at Bessemer Grange Play Centre, Southwark)

6 Play services

All children should have access to a range of good quality early years, play and out-of-school services such as play centres, holiday play schemes, adventure playgrounds, after-school clubs, playgroups, toy libraries and play buses.

Action points for play services

★ Respect the right of children to play freely and safely in a caring environment; a major part of the role of early years workers, play and out-of-school workers is to resource and facilitate the process of children's play.

★ Seek to provide good quality play environments and opportunities for children with a choice of activities, materials and time for free play.

★ Operate to national standards and clearly defined policies and procedures which have been set up with the participation of the children who use the services, parents and other carers, staff, and community representatives. Make these policies available in writing to all parties concerned, and review them regularly.

★ Work with children, parents and others to promote the importance of play and to safeguard and increase play opportunities within the community and more widely.

★ Ensure that children have ample opportunities to play outdoors.

'You should consult with children because it makes you better workers and makes the centre a better place to be for children.' (Member of the children's committee, Bessemer Grange Play Centre, Southwark)

Schools and play

All schools should support and facilitate children's play. Play and learning are not separate; play is part of learning and learning is part of play. Learning through play supports and enriches learning through formal education.

Action points for schools

★ Consult with children and develop policies for play so that children are able to benefit from a variety of good quality play opportunities in the nursery, classroom and playground.

★ Ensure that teachers and other school staff are appropriately supported to enable them to help children make the most of play opportunities during the school day.

★ Forge constructive links with providers of pre-school, after-school and holiday play services in your area to maximise play opportunities within your school and for your pupils.

★ Allocate sufficient time for breaktimes and playtimes, and avoid allowing other curricular demands to encroach on the time allocated to free play.

★ Improve your grounds so that they provide quality play experiences for pupils as well as support for the informal and formal curriculum.

★ Explore ways of maximising your resources for play outside school time, for example through the use of your premises by the community during the school holidays.

'Playtime is good, but it could be better by having more facilities and more room.'
(Scott Burroughs, age 11)

8 Safe play

Play opportunities should challenge and stimulate children's abilities but not threaten their survival or well-being.

Action points for play services

★ Create varied and stimulating environments for play, appropriate to your users' stage of development and physical capabilities, where every child will feel secure and be free from the risk of harm.

★ Recognise children's need to encounter and manage risk and challenge themselves. Provide for an acceptable level of risk-taking whilst removing known hazards.

★ Be aware of the requirements for registration under the Children Act 1989 and the duty to undertake risk assessments.

★ Ensure that staff and volunteers working with children have appropriate training, knowledge and experience for the duties and responsibilities expected of them.

★ Develop a child protection policy and procedures which are known to all management, staff, volunteers and parents.

★ Ensure that staffing ratios allow adequate supervision at all times.

★ Ensure that you know and conform to your legal responsibilities under health and safety legislation. Apply appropriate standards and codes of practice.

★ Increase levels of supervision in parks, and ensure that park staff have an understanding of play needs.

★ Ensure that all designated play areas are dog free.

'I go to a park which is full of broken glass and dog mess. It should have a clean up scheme because people could get hurt with the broken glass.' (Harry Dudley, age 10)

'I think that the local park isn't very safe because there is no park ranger or park keeper to look after the park so it does not get vandalised.' (Nicola Duff, age 11)

Special play situations

Hospital admissions, visits to a doctor, or a stay in temporary accommodation are some of the situations where children are in strange surroundings, perhaps experiencing fear, pain, anxiety and discomfort. They should be provided with play opportunities led by staff and volunteers who understand their special needs.

Action points for hospitals and health services

★ Acknowledge that play services are essential to quality care in hospitals, providing a normal experience in an otherwise abnormal environment and providing therapeutic play opportunities to enable children and their families to cope better with their hospital stay.

★ Provide play services at least from Mondays to Fridays, in all wards and units where children are cared for including intensive care units and teenage wards, and in out-patients and accident and emergency department waiting areas.

★ Acknowledge that qualified hospital play specialists, with appropriate resources, are an essential part of the ward team and of the community paediatric team offering appropriate play for the sick child at home.

★ Provide children with access to help from a specialist play therapist when needed.

Action point for temporary housing services

★ Ensure that you provide for children's play needs. Children living in temporary accommodation such as hostels and refuges, may have experienced trauma, violence, fear and uncertainty. In these circumstances, children and their families benefit enormously from good quality play opportunities.

Action point for other services

★ Children's play needs should be provided for in waiting areas in doctors' and dentist surgeries, health clinics, social services offices and anywhere else where children may be subject to extra stress.

'I felt lonely in hospital because there was no one to play with.' (Year 6 pupil, Good Shepherd School)

10 Playwork education and training

All playwork education and training should be flexible, adaptable, reflective of existing good practice in playwork and should involve a significant fieldwork practice component.

Action points for training providers

★ Develop playwork qualifications which are play specific and at a standard sufficient to confer a status equivalent to allied disciplines.

★ Provide access to a range of routes to a playwork qualification, including a route that allows for qualification by accreditation of past playwork practice. Ensure that these routes particularly meet the interests and needs of voluntary, temporary and part-time playworkers.

Action points for national policy makers

★ Develop a national peer-led endorsement process that applies to agencies offering training opportunities leading to a playwork qualification.

★ Ensure that any national endorsement body involves training bodies, fieldwork representatives and other relevant bodies. Ensure that appropriate standards are set for playwork in order to promote the education and training of playworkers, play development officers and play managers.

Action point for employers

★ Encourage people working with children in play and related settings to access good quality play education and training.

'A good playworker makes more good playworkers and more good playworkers makes a good adventure playground.' (Adventure playground user)